MELODIOUS MUSINGS OF LOVE

(AN ANTHOLOGY OF POEMS)
(PAPERBACK, 1ST EDITION, FEB 2023)

COMPILED AND EDITED BY :
DR. SONIA GUPTA

Dedicated to

Every  That

Knows to Love

Contents

Contents

Contents

Preface

"Love is the only reality and it is not a mere sentiment. It is the ultimate truth that lies at the heart of creation."
– Rabindranath Tagore

LOVE has been exquisitely defined by the renowned Indian poet and writer, Gurudeb Rabindranath Tagore that it is not merely a feeling, but the real truth that exists deep within the heart. LOVE is the most beautiful blessing that God has gifted to this world. Infect, LOVE is a necessity of living. Without LOVE, life is bare. LOVE is the reflection of the great Almighty. LOVE has been perceived in vivid forms by different people. Some consider it a symbol of romance, for some, it is merely a lust,for some, it is a divine feeling and for some, it is an ocean of pains. Whatever it is, it is unique in itself. LOVE is not an object to hold, capture or play with. It is a heart-to-heart bonding that is beyond any limits or boundaries.God has given us several occasions to celebrate the beauty of this life. And to express LOVE also, there are so many festivals in different religions. But Valentine's Day is one of the special occasions for lovers to show their LOVE toward their beloveds. Roses, sweets, gifts, treats, cards, letters, and a number of little gestures become part of this joyful occasion. Valentine's Day is celebrated throughout the world with high spirits and enthusiasm by every lover.

It is well said that poetry is the best mean to express our unsaid feelings and emotions with our silent pen and LOVE has been a favourite theme of poetry for poets for a long time in literature. Here, I can very well recall those heart-touching sonnets composed by the great legendary 'William Shakespeare' in the ode of Romeo & Juliet's LOVE stories. Today also, when we listen to those verses, a melody enchants our hearts.

Recently, after the successful publication of two anthologies of poems on WOMEN which were highly appreciated by readers and poets around the globe, poets approached me to publish another anthology on the theme LOVE/ VALENTINE in the joy of celebrating coming Valentine's Day on 14th February. That inspired me to think about this project and the result is in your hands, this beautiful anthology of Love poems "MELODIOUS MUSINGS OF LOVE". This is a collection of Fifty poems composed by Fifty poets from different regions of the world. While compiling these poems, I could feel that poets have expressed vivid shades and colors of LOVE through their beautiful verses that enchant melodious musings all around. That made an impression in my mind to choose the title as "MELODIOUS MUSINGS OF LOVE". The feelings hidden in these poems are unexplainable, which touch the heart of readers deeply and make them fall in LOVE with themselves and everyone around them. I am sure, after reading these verses, everyone will start composing the MELODIOUS MUSINGS OF LOVE and get drowned in the melody of LOVE forever and will feel this truth that VALENTINE'S DAY is not just a specific day but every day and each moment is a VALENTINE'S DAY. Let us all hold this book in hands and cherish these beautiful verses. Wish you all a magnificent, lovable, joyous and blissful VALENTINE'S DAY.

Dr. Sonia Gupta

Foreword

An Anthology Enchanting the Melody of Love

Dr. Shailesh Gupta Veer (Fatehpur, Uttar Pradesh, India)

If I am asked what is love? I will immediately reply that love is wider than the sky, and its definition is deeper than the ocean. Love is indeed very difficult to define, yet many definitions have been coined. The great American motivational writer William Arthur Ward explains love in very few words- "Love is more than a noun - it is a verb; it is more than a feeling - it is caring, sharing, helping, sacrificing." The expression of tender feelings of love has never been spontaneous, that's the reason the famous English religious poet and hymn-writer Frances Ridley Havergal declared- "Love understands love; it needs no talk."

Let's assume for a while that love needs no talk, yet our heart is always ready to give shape to infinite feelings of love. 'Talking about love' and 'talking in love' fill the heart with glee and bring a wondrous smile to the face. Love is the most beautiful feeling in this world. Without love, there is nothing. Love is life, and the motion of the world is incomplete without love.

Love is a happy form of union of two beautiful hearts. On the other hand, love is a sad form of separation also. The title makes it clear that the central theme of the anthology "Melodious Musings of Love" is 'Love'. According to great author Khalil Gibran- "Life without love is like a tree without blossoms or fruit." Many poems praising the glory of love enhance the beauty of the anthology. Many times, we take love very superficially, but it is not so. Beliefs of love can be of many colors, and their form can be different, but the essence of all is the same. There is no meaning of materiality without intimacy. The purity of love takes it to its highest form.

There are many feelings of love. These feelings themselves make capable interpretations of love. An excerpt from a sonnet by popular English poet of the Victorian era Elizabeth Barrett Browning cherished with deep feelings of love can be read here-

> "How do I love thee? Let me count the ways.
> I love thee to the depth and breadth and height
> My soul can reach, when feeling out of sight
> For the ends of being and ideal grace."

There has been some change in the concepts of love in every era, however, there has been no change in the universal concept of love. Innumerable golden stories of love from many parts of the world are recorded on the pages of history. There are also many vibrant stories of love in Indian tradition and literature, that makes us feel proud. Various colorful and magnificent poems by poets on an important subject like love add to the aura of the anthology and also present a captivating tableau of their love-related concept. The message of these poems is clear, the world is overflowing with the energy of love. This energy of love is the need of the times and society. Love is an important factor in creating a better world and in taking humanity to greater heights.

The anthology "Melodious Musings of Love" is a collection of fifty love poems composed by fifty poets. The poets have expressed vivid colors and shades of love through their verses which will be enchanted forever as melodious musings for the readers. As an editor, Dr. Sonia Gupta's efforts of presenting an anthology on such a beautiful theme called 'Love' from different poets throughout the world is highly appreciable. Hearty congratulations and best wishes to Dr. Sonia Gupta and all the eminent poets involved in it. I believe, it is a must-read anthology.

About Dr. Shailesh Gupta Veer

He is a poet, critic, reviewer, editor and multi-prize winner. He is a bilingual, writes in English & Hindi both. He is admin and moderator of various poetry groups on Facebook. He has edited about two dozen literary books and several magazines. His poetry has been published in various literary National and International magazines, journals, anthologies and websites. He has won many awards in the field of literature. His poems have been translated into Chinese, Greek, German, French, Azerbaijani, Arabic, Italian, Serbian, Croatian, Portuguese, Nepali, Punjabi & some other languages. He is the editor of Micro poetry Cosmos and the associate editor of The Voice of Creative Research. His love for human values, nature, philosophy and the spiritual world is insurmountable. He was declared a Literary Icon in December 2018 by TV program 'You and Literature Today' from Nigeria. His poems were read on 'The Dear John Show of Warrington,' England. He is an inspiration for the budding poets. He is PhD in Archaeology and is currently working as a Government Teacher.

CONTACT DETAILS:

- **Address:** 18/17, Radha Nagar, Fatehpur, UP, India - 212601
- **Mobile** : 9839942005
- **Email ID:** editorsgveer@gmail.com
- **Facebook ID:** https://www.facebook.com/shailesh.veer.39
- **Blog:** https://poetryshailesh.blogspot.com

Do Not Go Far out

You are calling

Heart is saying

Praying restart

Falling into you!

Wish to get you, darling!!

Magical charming face

Internal pious soul

Goal to get eternal

Grace is overall lyrical!

Wish to get you, darling!!

Without you

Creation is nothing

Everything sans elation

Do not go far out!

Wish to get you, darling!!

© Dr. Shailesh Gupta Veer

Heart Touching Verses Of Love

Donna McCabe (Rhondda, South Wales, UK)

Ah! love, what can we say about love? It makes us, it breaks us, it pulls us apart and puts us back together like little puzzle pieces. Yet we are never quite the same again. We have been changed by its overpowering influence. It shapes us and defines the very fabric of our everyday lives and relationships on every perceivable level. Deep in its complexities, quirkiness and logic just as we are as human beings.

The theme of the current anthology is valentine's day/ love. The history of this lovable occasion began as early as in the 14th century in England, with the tradition of exchanging love messages, called "valentines". With time moving on, this day is being celebrated with the exchange of objects like gifts, cards and sweets. Whatever it is, the feeling is the same, that is 'Love' that emerges straight out of a lover's heart touching the heart of another lover, thus forming an eternal bond. Love is a small word, but the depth of its existence can't be measured in words.

This beautiful anthology of love poems 'MELODIOUS MUSINGS OF LOVE' brings together a diverse and talented group of fifty poets from around the world. Each poet brings to these pages their own unique voice and familiarity on the subject of love and all the emotions it entails, culminating in a euphony of verse that is truly astounding and a pleasure to read again and again.

Dr. Sonia Gupta has already edited several anthologies, magazines, poems and write-ups of different poets and authors throughout the world. This anthology is one of her other achievements as an editor. A renowned author of sixteen independent poetry books in English and Hindi languages, she is swinging in the ocean of poetry with her wonderful contributions. Presenting different poets from different regions of the world on a single platform by Dr. Sonia Gupta is a highly tremendous job as an editor. I congratulate her for this wonderful achievement and all the beautiful souls included in this anthology who have given it the shape of a Lover's heart that enchants the souls around through these melodious verses. I am sure, the anthology will be well admired by the readers.

Biography of Donna McCabe

She is an established poet with over 20 years of experience whose vast variety of work has gained her multiple accolades within her field of literature over the years. From being published in journals, magazines and anthologies as well as being a highly respected admin in multiple social media groups, she is a regular contributor to literature. Besides this, she is an artist also. Her intricate wordplay displayed in her works has been personified by her past and concurrent experiences which include her hardships, trials and tribulations. Her lifetime admiration of reading and writing and love of art has steered her into an adventurous new direction of collaborations with an up-and-coming Canadian artist Ala Ilescu whose idiosyncratic mind and artistic works compliment the vivid images her narrative works paint. These collaborations have resulted in a beautiful book of poetry and artwork entitled "Explosion of Love" published on Amazon. Her creativity has also taken her onto other platforms in recent times, Using Instagram to reach out and display her love of writing, artwork, and love of the natural world to a wider audience. Her writings and interactions with the wider poetry communities there have helped her gain a good following and many features and awards too.

Email id- donna_salisbury@sky.com

Instagram page -@donnamccabe_

Facebook page- Poemsbydonnamccabe

Wounded Souls, Healing Hearts

My heart has been broken and shattered
But has been put back piece by piece
For I have found an understanding of the great depth
And an even deeper sense of peace.

The logic of love is a complex thing
The hearts reason is unknown
It is soft and adoring
But like a scorpion, a sting in its tail
Jealousy the green-eyed monster
Master of emotion.

Spears us when we least expect it
And shatters all our dreams
But with a little bit of magic
From another wounded soul
A broken heart is mended
And this I know.

© **Donna McCabe**

Poetry Illuminated By Love

Minko Tanev (Bulgaria)

Love is the greatest gift from God among the fruits of his spirit. In the "Hymn of Love" Saint Paul says: "if I do not have love, I am nothing." Those who love each other were said in ancient mythology to be struck by Cupid's arrow. According to legend, Saint Valentine used to give roses to young people from his garden. Between two lovers, a majestic feeling arose and following their example, hundreds of couples came from near and far to receive the blessing of the saint. The Valentine's Day was established in the year 496 by Pope Gelasius I, who included Saint Valentine among those names mentioned with respect by men, but whose deeds only God knows.

Today, literary competitions with Cupid prizes are organized in various countries, collections about love are published with selected works, such as the current volume "MELODIOUS MUSINGS OF LOVE" - an anthology of love poetry, compiled and edited by Dr. Sonia Gupta with 50 poets from all over the world.

Love is everywhere. We just have to enjoy it with the authors and their lyrical incarnations across the rivers, whose silver voices echo, and true enlightenment is in the heart of the beloved. Twinkling stars in the sky are witnesses of the eternal love affair.

God created the world with wisdom and power. For many, the most important thing is to find love, overcoming all barriers - racial, ethnic, cultural. The perfect bond of unity is in this string of life, in the voice of the heart, in the music rang out from the soul. In the secret waiting behind the lotus petals, in the garden of sublime flowers, a love fragrance is diffused. Continuous rediscovery of the beloved - when he looks at you, sparks burn in his eyes.

The romantic dream of meeting great love makes us feel alive, whole, gives us meaning and value. A sense that we have not lived in vain. Vows are spoken on top of the mountain, the divine aura of love shines. In sweet thoughts and dreams existence is delight and supreme bliss. A constant reinvention of the beloved.

Let's remember that love is not a feeling that is shown once a year on a holiday. Let's take advantage of every moment to tell the person close to our heart that we love them.

To live in love, it is not enough to be lucky to meet it, you also need the wisdom to make it a part of yourself. The time of closeness, in which you verbally open your soul to pour out and merge, is embodied in song and word in poetic pearls. In the land of love, in the heavenly ocean of eyes, the journey continues and fills us with light.

Dr. Sonia Gupta is a renowned poetess who has already established herself as an independent author of a total of sixteen books till date. As an editor, she has edited several anthologies, poems, magazines, and write-ups of many poets from the world. This anthology is one of her other achievements as an editor. The selection of poems by her has led to the compilation of a wonderful anthology that is well-appreciated. I congratulate Dr. Sonia Gupta and all the poets included in the anthology for their tremendous contribution. It is a must read anthology with beautiful verses and rhymes.

Biography of Minko Tanev

He is a poet, writer, author, editor and reviewer. He has authored six books and co-authored three bilingual books, poetry and haiku – in India with Stoianka Boianova. He has participated in over 60 International anthologies and publications with numerous awards and recognitions. He has edited over 70 books. He is in the European Top 100 of the most creative haiku authors. He has won several awards, "First World Poetry Competition of Newspapers and Televisions", 2020, China, Chinese International Zhengxin Poet Award, 2022, International Poetry Prize "Ossi di Seppia", 2023, Italy. He is a member of Union of the Bulgarian Writers, the Bulgarian haiku Union, the Haiku Foundation – USA, United Haiku and Tanka Society – UK, the World Haiku Association, Japan, Global Honorary Council of Federation of World Culture & Art Society (Singapore). He is a Philologist - Bulgarian language. He was a lecturer of Bulgarian language for foreign students – Medical University, Plovdiv.

- **Facebook ID:** https://www.facebook.com/minko.tanev.9
- **Email ID:** minkotanev@abv.bg

Bright Aura

The most lovely smile in the world
and your sublime gaze
I wanted to embody in verse,
to write with light.

I felt the tidal wave power
in your urge.
The dusk recognized my true face
and lifted us up.

Stellar blood filled ours hearts
the infinitude flames in love,
thousands of suns sparkle over us,
so we don't get lost.

© **Minko Tanev**

Acknowledgements

Gratitude seems to be a small word, but deep meaning it beholds. I usually hear these words – "If we say Thank you to someone, it means we are bowing our head in front of that Lord only". We can forget anything in life, but we should never forget to thank someone who has helped or motivated us in any way.

I am a medical professional, I never thought that one day I would become a writer, poet and author. It was merely a dream for me. But now it has become my passion, inspiration, and an integral part of my life. It's all by God's grace that he honoured me with such a unique gift.

First of all, I thank the Goddess of knowledge and wisdom 'Maa Saraswati', who gave me the strength to complete this work and encouraged me to pick up my pen to compile, edit, and prepare this anthology.

In the world, everything changes, but one thing that never ever changes is our parents. Heartfelt thanks to my parents for their faith and showering their infinite blessings on me. Special thanks to my father who has left this materialistic world attaining the embrace of the divine Lord. He had been my inspiration and will be forever and his teachings illuminate my life's pathway like an enlightening candle. Thankyou mom for being there throughout my work and for all your support and blessings.

Huge bundle of thanks to all the authors and poets, who have put their endless efforts by contributing their wonderful poems signifying the theme of this anthology. Most of the poets are much senior to me and I pay my regard and honour to all of them for their full cooperation from the day one of this project till the last moment, respecting my guidelines and instructions. Without all of you, this collection would not have been possible. Once again, my heartfelt thanks to all of you for your love, cooperation and encouragement.

A token of thanks to 'Dr. Shailesh Gupta Veer' sir for writing a wonderful foreword for this anthology and guiding at every step. Thank you sir for all your blessings and support.

My gratitude to the International poets 'Donna McCabe' from UK & 'Minko Tanev' from Bulgaria for taking out their valuable time in writing the reviews about this anthology despite their busy schedules. Thankyou both of you, your words have beautified our anthology.

Teachers are the selfless builders of our life, A word of thanks to all my respected teachers who always showed me the right path in my life and brimmed my heart with their blessings. Lovable token of gratitude to my brothers, sisters, and all family members for their love and support always. Friends are the precious ornaments gifted by God, who without any blood relation, make a bonding of forever relation. My regards and love to all friends far and near. Last but not least, it will be unfair if I forget to thank the Notion Press publication through which this book is going to be published. Thanks to entire team for the cooperation. Thank you, readers, fellow poets and friends for all your love and appreciation.

Dr. Sonia Gupta

Know About The Editor

Dr. Sonia Gupta (Mohali, Punjab, India)

She is a writer, poete, reviewer, editor and translator. She writes in English, Hindi, and Punjabi languages. By profession, she is a Dentist (MDS) with major specialization in Oral and Maxillofacial Pathology. Poetry is her passion. She writes in vivid genera of literature like poetry, stories, essays, letters, songs and many more. She has established herself as a renowned author after getting her Sixteen independent books published till date, out of which Ten are in English and Six are in Hindi language. Her English books are poetic collections entitled 'Spectrum of Life', 'Canvas of Life..With My Pen', 'Fountain of Inspirations', 'Meeting My Soulmate', 'Silent Verses', 'Mysterious Musings of Life', 'Agony of Life', 'Miracle of Virtues', 'Acrostic

Motivations', and 'There is No Darkness'. Her first English novel is coming soon. Her Hindi books include Five collections of poetry entitled 'Zindagi Gulzar Hai', 'Ummid Ka Diya', 'Kabhi Jalte Kabhi Bujhte Chirag','Kuch Ankahe Ehsas' and 'Prkriti Ki Gungunahat' and one collection of stories entitled 'Aadmi Bne Rehne Ka Dhong'.

Her literary journey continues with a great endeavour. She has gone through many ups and downs in her life that directed her vision toward suffering and she expresses that with her pen. Her writings reflect her closeness and deep love for nature, life, spirituality and humanity. For her, poetry is a God-gifted boon and she wishes to fly high wearing the wings of poetry. She has contributed to more than 100 National and International English anthologies so far. She is a regular contributor to various National and International magazines, newspapers and journals. She has translated many poems by other poets from different regions of the world into English, Hindi and Punjabi languages. She runs a blog about the Punjabi translation of English poems by different poets throughout the world. Her first poetry book in the Punjabi language is coming soon. She is an active member of various poetry groups on Facebook and has won several awards in writing competitions organized by these groups and other literary platforms. She won a Gold and Silver Medal in a Poetic world Cup contest held by Nigeria in Feb and May 2018 respectively, PRASANNA JENN MEMORIAL AWARD -2018 by the Asian Literary Society, and 5th rank in the International Essay writing competition on 'Skin complexion discrimination' organized by literary society, India in March 2018. One of her essays 'Our role & responsibilities toward nation was selected in a National essay writing competition and is a part of the book 'Youth as Nation Builders; a collection of 41 essays published by Lab Academia.

She is a famous name in Hindi literature also. She writes stories, essays, letters, articles, and vivid genera of Hindi poetry. Besides her independent Hindi books, her Hindi writings are part of several International and National anthologies, newspapers, journals and magazines. She has won many awards for her Hindi writings. Her many projects are underway.

Besides poetry, she is fond of painting, singing, cooking, teaching, reading, knitting, designing, stitching and embroidery. She has won many awards in Art competitions. Many of her paintings have been placed on the cover pages of various anthologies. Even she herself designed the cover pages of her two English anthologies entitled "Fountain of Inspirations" and "Canvas of Life…With My Pen". She is actively contributing to the literature via her literary YouTube channel, Facebook page, Blog and Instagram page.

Born and brought up in the family of well-educated people, Dr. Sonia is living her life with simplicity and a mission of doing something meaningful. She considers her family her biggest inspiration, who has always motivated her in each and every phase of her life. She feels proud to have such Grandparents who have enriched their children and grandchildren with ideal virtues and morals. Her grandfather is retired from the Indian Army and serves selflessly for society till today even being reached at the age of 97 Years and believes in doing his tasks on his own. Her grandmother left this materialistic world in 2020. She was a homemaker, who not only taught her Hindi language since her birth but also made her capable of learning other skills like cooking, knitting and embroidery. Dr. Sonia lost her father Late Sh. Devinder Kumar in 2019, who was retired as an English Lecturer from Govt. Senior Secondary School near their hometown. He lived his entire life for his children's bright future and it is his efforts that have let Dr. Sonia and her brothers achieve their goals. As a teacher, he was a renowned name in academics who guided a number of students who are working in well-recognized positions in society today. She is living her life following his teachings and footprints. Her mother, Mrs. Nirmal Devi is retired as a Private Secretary from the Higher Education Dept. Panchkula, Haryana. She is her best friend who has always motivated and accompanied her in her every adventure, whether related to her profession, passion or personal life. She has got two younger brothers, and she considers them the pillars of her life. She feels fortunate to find such brothers who have always stood beside her in even the darkest phases of her life, encouraging her to move ahead. One of her brothers works as a project manager at USA based company in Houston, Texas, USA. And youngest one is acting as a manager in MARUTI company, Manesar, Gurugram, Haryana. He is a professional singer also and is training his 8 - years old son in classical music. She feels blissful to get many teachers who not only taught her professional skills but also appreciated her passionate ventures and today also clap for her achievements. As a person, she is less talkative, simple, humble, hard-working and determined personality. She prefers to utilize every single moment in doing something meaningful rather than wasting in gossiping. She loves to work in a disciplined and organized way. She has completed her many poetry books while traveling to her work place. She is a deep believer in God and a great devotee of Lord Krishna. She is a member of the 'Mahila Mandal Sangeet Samiti' of many temples in her region and frequently participates in various religious events where she sings religious songs composed with her own pen. Her many religious books are in the process of publication.

Dr. Sonia Gupta is a renowned name in her professional field also. She is working as an Associate Professor in the Oral Pathology Dept. at a Dental College in Mohali. She is also pursuing a fellowship program in Forensic

Odontology by the Indian Board of Forensic Odontology. She serves the community as a doctor by providing dental care. She has got several scientific publications in PubMed and Scopus-indexed National and International Journals with the first authorship and many more are under review. She is also working on three textbooks on her subject of specialization. She is acting as a reviewer of various Medical and Dental Journals. She actively takes part in various conferences, workshops, community health programs, and events and has presented several research papers and posters. She is a dedicated academician with a goal of making her students excel in their subjects and in developing their multitalented skills. She is enjoying her professional as well as literary journey full of passion and mission.

CONTACT DETAILS:

- **ADDRESS-** #95/3, Adarsh Nagar, Dera Bassi, Dist: Mohali, Punjab-140507, India.
- **MOBILE-** 6280420736
- **FACEBOOK ID** - 100004964983747@facebook.com
- **FACEBOOK PAGE** - https://www.facebook.com/sonia4840/
- **BLOG** - http://drsoniablogspot.blogspot.in/
- **PUNJABI TRANSLATION BLOG** - http://passionatepunjabijourney.blogspot.com/
- **E MAIL** -drsoniagupta82@gmail.com
- **YOUTUBE CHANNEL** https://www.youtube.com/channel/UCKF2jM5P8VDjZ9fBZLBTRH
- **INSTAGRAM ID-** https://instagram.com/gdrsonia?igshid=YmMyMTA2M2Y=

Melodious Musings Of Love

O' my Amour, your love is something special,
Each and every moment, it brings a miracle,
I get mesmerized drowning in its nectar,
It blooms in my life's garden like a blooming flower.

Everywhere I listen to melodious musings,
In the ocean of romance, my feet start dancing,
Without any reason, my face starts smiling,
Like a diamond, my eyes start glittering.

I cherish a paradise embraced in your arms,
I forget the whole world lost in love charm,
Even hot scorching sunrays appear like love shower,
Deserts also appear to be green forever.

You are my life, I love you my Amour,
You have given me a reason to live my dear,
I am your sun, you are my sunshine,
Let us stay together, O' my valentine.

© Dr. Sonia Gupta

List Of Poets

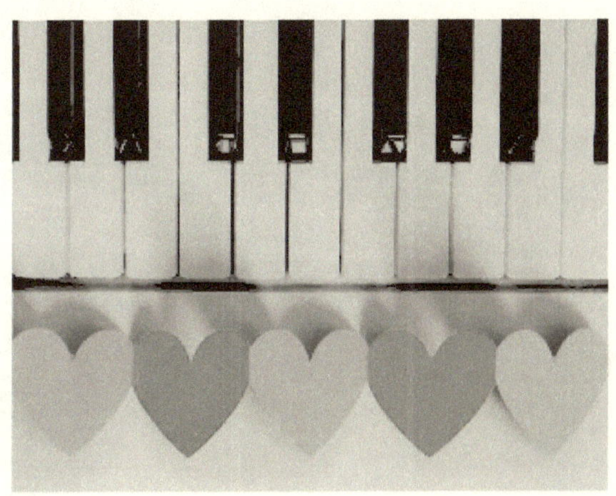

MELODIOUS MUSINGS OF LOVE

*An Anthology of Poems
(Paperback, 1ˢᵗ Edition, February 2023)
Compiled & Edited BY
Dr. Sonia Gupta*

1. My Love

That white ocean...with silver waves, I love
A little deeper...
The intense depth
I wish to sink into a world different...

Maybe the one who yearned for
A step, stepping in
The river of nectar
The honey to be sipped
Sip by sip…

The taste of heaven
A touch ...drenched in love
On that bed of snow
Pale but warm
An embrace a dwell
For lifetime
A stroll ...a mount....a ride
Of ecstasy
With bliss, wish, a desire...

© Aarti Mittal

Aarti Mittal (Mumbai, Maharashtra, India)

aarti.amittal@gmail.com

She is a bilingual poet who writes in English & Hindi languages. She writes short skits with morals for children. She follows the religion of humanity, compassion and love and tries to spread the same. She believes that her writings can win hearts and help to bring some change to make this world a better place. Her writings also include themes based on women's empowerment and child exploitation. She is B.A. B.Ed and pursuing M.A. Currently, she is working as a teacher.

2. My Precious Gift

I received the present, the beautiful gift you present',
I read the heart-melting message, you sent,
I am still expectant, for that is not sufficient,
Without you my JEWEL, I am incomplete and deficient.

My Precious Gift, to me the ALMIGHTY presented this Painite,
Many wonderful women have done noble things,
But you surpass them all, your beaming smile,
Drained my well of worry, too hurry to say sorry,
See! The sea of sorrow dried up when she showed up.

A charming face is fleeting and beauty is deceptive,
But you are altogether beautiful, there is no flaw in you,
Oh my love, how wonderful you are! Glitter than Gold,
You humble my heart with kindness, your brilliance is untold.

My Precious God Given Gift, my Valentine,
How sweet are your honeyed lips? Better than wine,
Please stay with me always, please forever be mine.

© Ajayi Oluwasegun Samson

Ajayi Oluwasegun Samson (Osogtbo, Osun, Nigeria)

ajayiolusegun49@gmail.com

He is a poet and a creative writer. Poetry is his passion. He writes poems, essays and stories since secondary school. He has won several prizes and awards during his schooling both at the National and Local levels, in debate competitions and essay writing. He is an active member of several poetry groups on Facebook. Presently, he is pursuing Nursing.

3. O' My Lovely Bud

O' my lovely bud,
I wish you to be my flower,
You are the one who can decorate my desolate bower,
If I am not your sun, moon is not far from your glance.

My eyes always stuck to your face,
Waiting for the veil of pink petals to be opened
Winter's night terrifies me,
As my flower is beyond my view.

You have many a hue,
Which enhances your beauty,
The only thing that can overcome my fear.
O' my dear! O' my dear! O' my dear.

© Alok Mishra

Alok Mishra (Sitapur, Uttar Pradesh, India)

alokk2129@gmail.com

He is an award-winning bilingual (English & Hindi) poet, critic, reviewer and editor. He is Admin of a poetry group "Literature Lover Association" on Facebook. His poems are published in several National and International anthologies, newspapers and magazines. He has edited 6 anthologies of English poems. He is M. Phil in English and presently working as a Government teacher. He is also an astrologer.

4. Let's Stop the Light

O' my valentine…
Let's stop the light at the door,
Now the darkness is coming to us,
It is taking us away from the light.

Old days seemed full of pain,
You did not come often to keep your promises,
And since you were a bit sensible,
Life had become so sweet.

Let us stop the light at the door itself,
The plains of our memories will start from here,
Where the ruins of love end,
Endlessly.

© Anil Gupta

Anil Gupta (Ujjain, Madhya Pradesh, India)

guptamedicose14@gmail.com

He is a bilingual poet and writer who writes in English and Hindi languages. He has authored a book entitled "History of Ujjayini and greatness of Simhastha". He is an active member of various poetry groups on Facebook and participates in many poetry contests. His writings are part of several National and International magazines, newspapers and anthologies. He has won several awards for her poetry. He is an editor of the weekly magazine 'Mahakal brahman. He is also a Senior Correspondent of Doordarshan Bhopal Canter –Ujjain. He is MSc, LLB, and M.J.M.C. Currently, he is working as a Pharmacist and Journalist.

5. Love Finds Serenity

Roses from the garden of my fantasy land,
Shower you with the fragrance of beauty,
Mystify and amaze with the image of being together,
Let's celebrate love blissfully.

As we meet our souls' desires selflessly,
Hurdles can't stop us from loving unconditionally,
It spreads out the roots deep down and survives,
Love is a deep expression of mental freedom.

That is mistaken as the physical urge at times,
True love frees the spirits,
Love is never a burden but a feeling of solidarity,
That never coops the inner strength for material pursuits.

It kindles the serenity unreservedly,
Such love is divine and beyond explanation,
It is more magical than physical,
O' dear, your love is special.

© Anju Charanjith

Anju Charanjith (Muscat, Oman)

anjucharanjith@gmail.com

She is a poet and writer. She is an active member of various poetry groups on Facebook and participates in many poetry contests. Her writings are part of several National and International magazines, newspapers and anthologies. She has won several awards for her poetry. She is a TESOL graduate and is pursuing the International PG Diploma in TESOL/ TEFL program. Presently she works in the Sultanate of Oman.

6. That Dark Evening

The sun casts variable shadows,
On the hushed waters, as it became deeper,
And descended sharply on the placid lake.

Clouds stood restful,
In the skies above, even,
as I recounted.
The happy day that was…

The evening dusk slithered,
Coalescing into dark sheets,
Engulfing us in a strange,
Moonless night.

Suddenly, in the dark, I saw,
That weren't we just pretending.

© Dr. Balesh Jindal

Dr. Balesh Jindal (Delhi, India)

jindalbalesh@yahoo.co.in

She is a renowned artist with a creative portfolio of art, poetry and photographs. She has published three poetry books; a coffee table book 'A Hundred Dreams', 'Dear Father' and 'The Reluctant Doctor a Memoir'. She is a physician by profession; a graduate of the prestigious Lady Hardinge Medical College in Delhi and has had a professional medical practice for the last forty years. She has received several awards in her professional and literary fields.

7. A Lover's Quarrel

Memory oft softens lover's sullen face
Crimson quarrel awaits the shower cool.
It mollifies his brawl with the world
Like the carcass is salvaged for its hide.

The hooves are given by the swain
He feels fluffy beneath the flesh of love.
They sit side by side in cooing awe
They knee together on other occasions.

Like the fracas between blonde & brunette
The next moment they peck at each other.
The lover strides athwart choking humidity
To reconcile to the sulky world he loves.

© Basudev Paul

Basudev Paul (Malbazar, West Bengal, India)

basudevpaul01@gmail.com

He is a poet, writer and author. His poetry is a psalm; a sacred song of his life felt at the gloaming of his career. His poetical composition aiming at the worship of God chants as a canticle for humanity. He has published one English poetry book; "The Permanent Transient". He is M.A. in English and has worked as a teacher with thirty-seven years of teaching experience.

8. A Tube Rose

I was offering you a glass of water,
You asked for the flower,
I was wearing on my hair a small tube rose,
You insisted on only that one I wore.

Gladly you tucked it on your shirt and went away,
Wearing my heart on your heart,
Did you know I was going with you?
Over the years is the tube rose still there?

How many times has that scene been replayed?
Through the memory's window?
Every time I see a tube rose,
Or a rose or any other flower.

I feel overwhelmed by the fragrance,
As it is not you or me,
But our everlasting love....
That filled the small tube rose.

© Bharati Nayak

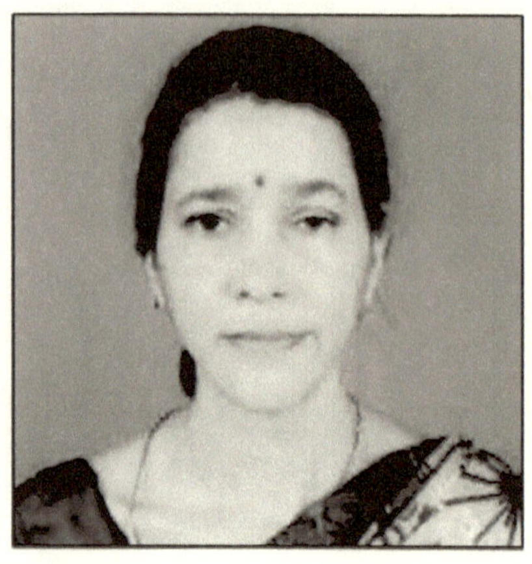

Bharati Nayak (Bhubaneswar, Odisha, India)

bharati1962@rediffmail.com

She is a bilingual (English & Odia) poet, writer, translator and editor. She has so far published two Odia poetry collections, one book of translation of South African poetess Adiela Akkoo's book 'Lost in A Quatrain' into Odia, two English poetry collections as sole author and six books as co-author with other poets. She is a postgraduate in Political Science. She is retired as Under Secretary from the Revenue & Disaster Management Department, Odisha.

9. The Kiss

Your kiss...
Tore up the skies,
In thunderous applause and lightning flashes;
Going right down to the root,
Of the earth, I stood on,
Shaking me up,
Out of my safe reverie, into a storm,
Casting me away, to a place,
Hitherto unknown ...

I swam in the depth of the ocean,
Floated with waves,
And the clouds in the sky,
Flew with the birds,
Swept away in a tornado of emotions,

And yet,,
It was my elixir of life,
Was it a miracle, or a mirage?
Your Kiss...

© Ipsita Ganguli

Ipsita Ganguli (Kolkata, West Bengal, India)

ipsitaganguli@gmail.com

She is a business consultant at sunrise and poet, travel writer and heritage, and art enthusiast at sunset. Her poems have been published in several e-magazines and anthologies. She is also one of the main characters of the poetry film 'Kolkata Cocktail'. She has also conducted a series of online Talk Shows entitled 'Cafe Conversations' as well as curated offline Poetry events for Kolkata Literary Meet. She is a recipient of many literary Awards. She has two independent compilations of poems.

10. Once Upon

Once upon a valentine's day, I gave you a smile,
Now, your eyes greet me,
People's tasteless sighs mould my mood,
And, red roses convey their bleeding emotions,
For getting used or unused in strongly doubtful ways.

My love for you remains the same,
Valentine's days taste changes,
We cope with reliabilities, mere unconditional conditions.

I've learned to shape or reshape your image in me,
Because love matters a lot to us,
Let your lips get mingled with the smile that I give.

Once upon a valentine's day, you met me in silence,
Now, I remain silent when you pass by,
Only horribly comfortable silence everywhere.

Tears, fears, and dearest memories maintain silence,
To place us on our self-designed royal roads to happiness.

© *Bipul Chandra Kalita*

Bipul Chandra Kalita (Nagaon, Assam, India)

bipulkalita074@gmail.com

He is a trilingual poet who writes in Assamese, Hindi and English language. He has authored three books. He has edited many journals and literary anthologies. His writings have been published in many National and International magazines, newspapers and anthologies. He has authored nearly 26 Assamese plays. He is M.A. in English and currently working as a post-graduate teacher.

11. Celestial Valentine

A cool soothing shade above the ground,
A footfall in the air unheard of esoteric sound,
Some call it euphoria, others feel ecstasy,
But to me, it's love's serene efficacy.

An ethereal being or non-mundane entity,
Sitting atop the moon's crest a sempiternal beauty,
Joy personified or bounty of divine boon,
Devotees of love with her are in tune.

The epitome of elegance the sparkle of stream,
Gazing at her aura seems a colourful dream,
Draped in silver she ever-remains sedentary,
Riding bulbous clouds trailing in mystery.

Who is she, a fairy or spirit, none can say,
This secret will be revealed by a lover someday,
Who is she, a deity or a nymph or a flying beauty?
Celestial Valentine or a real physical entity.

© Birendu Kumar Sinha

Birendu Kumar Sinha (Patna, Bihar, India)

birenduksinha14@gmail.com

He is a freelance journalist, short story writer and poet. He has authored two poetry books namely 'Fragrance of earth' and 'Symphony of love'. He is an active member of various poetic forms on Facebook. He has won several awards for his poems. He served as a English lecturer and Senior Management Officer at State Bank of India.

12. Your Arrival

A sweet melodious sound
Of illusive rhyme
Flows silently
On a solitary crossroad.

The painful time scattered
In the screech of an owl
The void greed of the heart
Spreads the fragrance of golden Shower tree.

A rhynchostylis retusa
Makes spring's heart crazy
A shower of rain
Draws a rosy shadow of deceptive rainbow.

The lamentation of Indian Nightingale
Speaks your arrival
The leafless tree
Reflects greenery
a soft hug of warm desires.

© Boby Borah

Boby Borah (Tinsukia, Assam, India)

bobyborah30@gmail.com

She is a poet and author. She has authored three books and edited several magazines. Her poems and articles are published in several newspapers in Assam. She has been awarded several awards in her professional and literary journey. She is M.A. in literature, Founder / Principal of Shankardev Shishu Niketan school. She is also the president of Doom Dooma Mahila Samiti and secretary of Sundoram Kobi Sanmilan.

13. Lover's Gift

At the onset of spring,
Lover's gift it brings,
Come to my heart's garden,
To turn it into a real Eden.

Spreading shivers of joy,
Come dear let's enjoy,
This scintillating evening,
Special euphonic feeling.

As you come methinks my love,
Make me shy by sweet love dove,
On your lips, crescent moon,
Intoxicated I just swoon.

No reason I seek or ask,
The excited mind goes blank,
Basking in thy warmth,
Subsidies heart's storm.

© B. S. Saroja

B. S. Saroja (Bangalore, Karnataka, India)

bssaroja1953@gmail.com

She is a poet, writer and author. Her poems and writes have been published in many anthologies, magazines, and periodicals. Poetry is her lifelong passion. She is also a social worker. She is a postgraduate in Kannada and a graduate in Science and a Diploma holder in Commerce and is retired as a personal secretary to the Managing Director of a business organization.

14. I Surrender

I surrender everything to you
I know you would do all good
The highest pleasure can be attained
It's the gift of God reserved for us
That we can't misuse if I am true.

Together brings pleasure to everyone
Even wave giggles with the songs of birds above
Loneliness essential for supreme creation
But someone was there beside for the ignition
That may be you or I am for you.

Massacre managed with Godly love
Everyone in the world wants peace, harmony, serenity
Why does ego play sometimes between us?
That can be melted with understanding, caress for tomorrow
This way we shall weave another story.

© Damodar Boruah

Damodar Boruah (Dergaon, Assam, India)

damodarboruah14@gmail.com

He is a multi-award-winning poet, writer and translator at the National and International levels. He has composed more than five hundred poems to date. He is an active member of various poetry groups on social media. His recent book 'From A Father to A Daughter...to touch the sky!' has become a great hit. His motto: 'Create Farmers, Create Entrepreneurs, Create Markets, Create Stories.' is widely accepted among many stakeholders. He holds a degree of B.Sc(Hons), GNIIT and DBM. By profession, he is a small tea grower and farmer.

15. Blissful

My heart goes beating faster
With rain nonstop pattering
My courtyard starts dancing
With silvery anklets tinkling;

You dance and sing on a spree
In frenzy to mesmerize many;
Somewhere in the darkest corner
A poor soul searches for his Destiny.

I let go wealth, fame and name;
Short-lived all can't sustain me;
In your sweet thoughts & reveries
Exist I to enjoy the bliss supreme.

© Dasharath Naik

Dasharath Naik (Sundargarh, Odisha, India)

dasharath23664@gmail.com

He is a poet, writer and an editor. Poetry is his passion and he writes for pleasure. His main motto is to spread peace, love, and humanity through his poetry. He is the Admin of various poetry groups on Facebook. He has contributed to several anthologies, magazines, and journals, both Nationally and Internationally. He is M.A. & M.Phil. in English. Currently, he is working as a Reader (SS) in English.

16. Eye Contact

It's always evening that brings you in, so close intimate,
A big fool within prompts me ever you to tease,
So that Glow- worms of your silence would flounder about me,
Does sizzling, fiery, scorching eye contact send, Fire – flies' desire.

Will slowly illumine dark caves of body which is depressive,
I am trying out my tolerance , persistently waiting, posited patience,
To smell aroma of smile, Pollens of love me encircling,
I know already that nearness, Exhibition of something you texting,

Our eye – contact, pair of blue eyes,
surely close our distancing,
Alleviate our multitude of dry emotions,
Fulfil long awaited desires.

We join and reunite with huge effect of love, togetherness,
I cannot believe this,
You are actually looking into my eyes,
And… creating a sweet miracle.

© Dr. Gangalaxmi Patnaik

Dr. Gangalaxmi Patnaik (Bangalore, Karnataka, India)

gangalaxmi80@gmail.com

She is a bilingual poet who writes in English and Odia languages. She is an active member of various literary groups on Facebook. She writes in vivid genera of poetry. Her writings are part of several National and International magazines, newspapers and anthologies. She actively participates in various poetry recitation fests. She has won several awards in English literature. She is M.A and PhD in English and a former Associate Professor in English.

17. Separation

The spur I was separated
From my beloved
I was all alone
Useless it is to be born.

Where shall I go now?
My life to whom I owe?
My thoughts crystallised
My imaginations paralysed.

My emotions struck
I was transfixed
I was like a fish out of water
Like a soap without lather.

Oh my lover
I still love you
How can I forget you?
Ever cheering, ever adoring, ever new.

© Gargi Saha

Gargi Saha (Varanasi, Uttar Pradesh, India)

gargi.paik@gmail.com

She is a creative writer since her childhood. She has published two poetry books namely 'The Muse in My Salad Days' and 'Letters to Him'. Recently she received the Rabindranath Tagore Memorial Award and the Independence day award for poetry. She is a member of various poetry groups on Facebook. She is M.A and M.Phil. in English. Presently she edits several scientific research papers.

18. Delicate Rose

A delicate rose blooms to him,
In his hands it seems fragile sin,
However, when he opens its petals,
Its dazzling fragrance kettles.

As much as he tries to discard her,
Completely fascinated by the aroma per,
Such delicate flower catches his eyes,
Keeping it on his own garden highs.

The morning saw astonishing both in pair,
Willing to spreading famous scent in the air,
Or maybe , together matched to fly height,
To their dream, joined the supremacy tonight.

© Gelda Castro

Gelda Castro (Reo de Janerio, Brazil)

gel2015c@gmail.com

She is a poet, writer and artist. She started writing poetry in English few years ago. She is actively participating in several literary groups, anthologies and Poetic Festivals. She has written more than a thousand poems. Poetry is her motto as an antidote to the ills of the world. She graduated in Portuguese-English languages and is currently working as a teacher.

19. Together Not Just Valentine

Sun has stars, Moon has rays, Ocean has waves
In Nature none is forlorn
With you, in you, I need not yearn
As have whole universe in my arms

You, Me part of HIS cosmic design
HIS grace making us each other's Valentine
Masculine, Feminine power blending into one
Shiva-Shakti, cosmic power couple, our revered ideals

Together, not just Valentine, but are a force
Unboxing, reinforcing energy source
Marching forward on terrain smooth and coarse
Transcending hand-in-hand on divine liberation course

© Dr. Hitendra Mehta

Dr. Hitendra Mehta (Mumbai, Maharashtra, India)

hitendramehta@rediffmail.com

He is an IIM L Alumnus and a Polymath - poet, artist, social activist and socio-economic thinker, He was a semi-finalist in International Poetry Contest, and Silver Medallist in the All India Drawing Competition. He has authored two books. He is a member of the World Human Rights Protection, Commission, a volunteer at the UN Online Volunteer Program, and featured in Gujarati Midday and Tata Sky interview. He is retired as CEO from Aifso Technologies.

20. Soul and Oversoul

Only because I connect through the soul,
Which I see in your eyes...
I need say nothing to you,
For You know me all— because it's all in the eyes.

And I know that you can see all of me …which you truly can,
The good, the bad, the ugly and beyond.
It doesn't even matter because I know..
That you will love me, whatsoever.

You have taught me to love myself; all of me.
Because all of me and all of you are divine and perfect,
Pious, pure, untouched, and unconditional, beyond the ordinary.

The fiery spark of your magnetic presence pulls me toward you,
Like a little phoenix pulled toward the cosmos,
With that invisible thread of love and light,
Connecting the Soul with the Oversoul.

© Lakshmi Ajoy

Lakshmi Ajoy (Mumbai, Maharashtra, India)

ashwini04182@gmail.com

She is a writer, artist, photographer, solo traveller, adventure sports enthusiast, mountaineer and social worker. She is a member of various poetry groups on Facebook and has won several awards. Her aim is to spread happiness and joy all around and help others realize the value and essence of life. Writing helps her to give wings to her imagination and live her dreams. Currently, she works as a spiritual healer and entrepreneur.

21. Valentine Vagaries

Had I known your gaze would melt my heart
I should have looked the other way.
Had I known the pangs of your absence
I would have traded my soul for wings.

When I saw you spying on me as I climbed the sink
I slipped and fell, you caught me under your spell;
When your secretary pursued and cornered you
The world ended, ending my love for you.

I'll whisper your name in every flow'r
I'll hug you in the warmth of Zephyr;
I'll paint our love on the canvas of the sunset
I'll always remember that I will love you forever.

Husband's cable read: "Doubt thou the stars are fire...."
Leilani smiled all day; giggling, she bragged to me:
"My Benny is so sweet, he writes like a poet"
Yes, dear, I smiled;, at Ophelia from Hamlet.

© Madelyn Fernandez-Marcelino

Madelyn Fernandez-Marcelino

(Barotac Viejo, Iloilo, Philippines)
christyballadares@gmail.com

She is a writer, poet and author. She is a passionate lover of nature. She is an active member of various literary groups on Facebook and has won several awards in poetry. Her poems are placed in several National and International newspapers, anthologies and magazines. She holds a B.A. degree.She is a teacher and speech coach.

22. Deep Inside

Deep inside…
I feel, I need to be with you,
You care for me though aware of my disabilities,
Loving me as I am…ever supportive.

Sharing my thoughts and ideas,
Clearing the arising doubts,
Your talks keep me awake. Day and night,
Your voice… Brings flutters in my heart.

Your captivating smile.. Showers happiness,
I wish to hold you in my arms,
To ward off your fatigue and evil eyes,
I would rest my head on your shoulder forgetting myself.

I enjoy the moonlight and the sunshine remembering you,
Every passing day we spend together…is a pleasure,
Be my Valentine dear,
Today and forever.

© Madhuri Kulkarni

Madhuri Kulkarni (Bangalore, Karnatka, India)

gouriraj69@gmail.com

She is a bilingual poet who writes in English and Kannada languages. Writing is her passion. She is an active member of various literary groups on Facebook and has won several awards in poetry. Her writes are published in National and International magazines, newspapers and anthologies. Talkative by nature, she wishes to spread love and positivity through her poetry. She holds a degree of Masters of Commerce. Currently, she runs a playschool for poor kids.

23. No need to Say

I can listen to your heart,
No need to say that you love me.
I can read your eyes,
No need to say you are always searching for me.

I can listen to your untold words,
No need to say what you want to tell me.
Your open arms always ask,
No need to say come to me.

When I am in pain your actions say,
No need to say you care for me.
What do you want to eat,
No need to say to me.

You enjoy spending time together,
No need to ask me.
You can't stay away or alone,
No need to say to me.

© *Manaswinee Dash Panigrahi*

Manaswinee Dash Panigrahi

(Bhubaneswar, Odisha, India)

gouriraj69@gmail.com

She is a poet by passion. She is an active member of various literary groups on Facebook and has won several awards in poetry. Her writes are published in National and International magazines, newspapers and anthologies. She wishes to spread love and peace through her poetry. She is a homemaker and holds a degree of M.Sc. and M.Phil in Environmental Sciences.

24. Love on the Walls of Heaven

Fragments of mirages appeared on the walls of the earth,
Start a love affair framed in the story,
It seems that longing always sets the whole body on fire,
Will the history of perfection repeat itself?
Convince me to promise the bright moon,
To be with you forever only death will part.

Sunlight lights the path of our love,
Our dream is to fall in love in life,
That is colorful like a Ferris wheel,
Our conscience is wrapped in a faith that is immune,
It is not uncommon for laughter and tears to accompany each other,
But the various love writings are not just dead letters.

The word love is not an empty sound,
To be sown by children and grandchildren in the spring,
In the boat of love and soul, we sail,
Reach out holding each other defy the waves,
Cling tightly all in divine love.

© Mário de Oliveira Pires

Mário de Oliveira Pires (Dilli, Timor Leste)

marioolive34@gmail.com

He is a poet, author, writer and a translator. He is a member of several poetry groups on Facebook and has won many awards in poetry contests. His poems are placed in several anthologies, magazines and newspapers. He has worked as a translator in the communications department of the Dili archdiocese.

25. Virtuous Flames

Superscribe her as the effulgent or shimmering moon
Whatever attributes one proffers
The bard's muse or painter's boon
Nightingales crush or nights brightest wonder.

The sun doesn't claim that all her silver is mine
When waves rush to the shore, swelling with tidal love
The ocean never claims that "you are mine"
A progenitor never demands love for love.

From the pupil, a pedagogue expects nothing
When you find any love sans conditions
Wrap it under your wings and feel like a colorful spring
For in this benumb world of contrition.

Even time halts to applause such rare gems
Never let it go
An eternal virtuous flames
Beyond the time it flows and glows.

© Mousumee Baruah

Mousumee Baruah (Gurgram, Haryana, India)

mousumimamu@rediffmail.com

She is a bi-lingual freelance writer and poet. Many of her poems and short stories are published in various National & International literary platforms, anthologies, blogzines, etc. She has won several awards in her literary journey. She is the author of the poetry collection, "The Castaway". She is a Master's in English. She worked as a lecturer.

26. Love Forever

Our love is blossoming in endless forms,
Our togetherness forever,
Memoirs of every life, every moment,
Strung into a necklace worn around your slender neck.

The priceless gems shine on forever,
You emerge in every dream,
A silhouette clads in celestial light,
Together we float on the stream of time.

The coy embrace, the tearful farewells,
Each time it was renewed love,
A treasure of tender memories I cherish,
Love that will never wither, never perish.

© Pradnya Surve

Pradnya Surve (Mumbai, Maharashtra, India)

pradnya1260@gmail.com

She is a poet and writer. She is an active member of various literary groups on Facebook and has won several awards in poetry. Her writes are published in National and International magazines, newspapers and anthologies. She wishes to spread love and peace through her poetry. She is a homemaker and holds a degree of Postgraduate in Child Development and Family Relations.

27. A Wonder

Chaos in life was reverberating continually,
That my dreams were numb to find a path in the dark,
Expectations were buried under the sands of time,
Till someone knocked at the door of my heart.

Promised to accumulate my fragile pieces,
Gathering those made me a whole,
Years of suffering treated to heal,
Isn't it a wonder! an unknown feeling touched my core.

An unseen force connected our souls,
The universe is submerging into an endless flow,
Where a million morai of lights started to light up,
Removing gloomy clouds, revealing the beauty of love.

© Pragyan Parimita Nanda

Pragyan Parimita Nanda (Guwahati, Assam, India)

m123.nanda@gmail.com

She is a trilingual creative writer in Odia, Hindi, and English languages. She writes in different journals both Print and magazines, plus on online platforms Instagram and Facebook. She is a homemaker, a trained journalist, a voracious reader, and a passionate writer who loves to travel and explore new places. She is M. A in Journalism.

28. Love Is Metaphor

Love is seraphic and angelic,
No wry, worry, no sneer, jeer.
Love's place; paradise atmospheric,
Lovely love is pleasure and cheer.

Noble love is wiser than philosophy,
Lighter than power though mighty,
Being sagacious and judicious theosophy,
Abler than strength having the ability.

Flame-coloured are love's wings,
Lips as sweet as honey,
Coloured like flame its body spring,
Breathe like frankincense sunny.

Love makes delicate flush of pink,
Like the flush in the face of the bridegroom.
Love appears crimson colour on the lips quick.
Age only knows love as never dies in the tomb.

© Prasanna Bhatta

Prasanna Kumar Bhatta (Berhampur, Odisha, India)

prasanabhatta1@gmail.com

He is a budding writer who began writing in 2021. He is a member of various poetry groups on Facebook and actively participates in various poetry contests. He has won several awards for his poetry. He has co-authored one poetry book 'KAVYA KUMBHA' which is recognised in Indian book of records and is well accepted by the readers. He is M.A, M. Ed and is retired as principal of GVJC College.

29. Extortion Day

Love is friendship that has caught fire,
Love is composed of a single soul inhabiting two bodies,
I perceive one duty, and that is to love,
I need you like a heart needs a beat.

Women are meant to be loved, not to be understood,
Love all, trust a few, do wrong to none,
You call it madness but I call it love,
A life lived in love will never be dull.

We love it because it's the only true adventure,
One happiness in life, is to love and be loved,
Today is valentine's day, I like to call it, Extortion day,
Love is what makes the ride worthwhile.

We are most alive when we are in love,
There is no charm equal to the proclivity of the heart,
True love stories never have endings,
We love it because it's the only true adventure.

© Dr. Prasanna Kumar Mohapatra

Dr. Prasanna Kumar Mohapatra

(Odisha, Bhubaneshwar, India)
pkmo.kbl@gmail.com

He is a budding writer who started his poetic journey 1 year ago. He is a member of various poetry groups on Facebook and has achieved a lot of recognitions of his poetry. He is a founder of a poetry group, 'United Poets@ Heart'. He is encouraging many poets and writers through his group. He is post graduate and M.Sc in Applied Mathematics. He is retired from LnT company in Odisha and working in LIC company at present.

30. Love's Light

Love is here, love is there,
Up in the sky, on a moonless night,
And below the earth,
In the lightless caves.

This light saves you, me and all,
From dying unconsciously,
In an otherwise darkening life.

This light is of love,
And love lightens life,
Here on this earth,
There beyond this world,
Everywhere and all around.

Let love's light burn here,
To brighten our atmosphere,
And enlighten the inner sphere,
It will help us over there.

© Promila Punnu Bhardwaj

Promila Punnu Bhardwaj

(Shimla, Himachal Pradesh, India)
bhardwajpamela@gmail.com.

She is a bi-lingual poet who writes in English and Hindi Languages. She has authored three English and two Hindi poetry books. She is an active member of various literary groups on Facebook and participates in several poetry contests. She has won many awards for her poetry. Her poems have been published in National and International newspapers, literary magazines and anthologies. She is M. A. in English Literature and is retired General Manager, Industries Department of H.P. Government.

31. In His Limped Eyes

In his limpid eyes...
You can see the whole sky,
The moon, the stars
The wounds and scars.

You can see his soul..
Beautiful and pure,
You can see the whole universe,
When his eyes converse.

You can see a rainbow or two,
When he sparkles through,
The whole universe dances,
Floating in his love.

His greenish blue eyes...
Behold a beautiful smile,
My lifeline...
His limpid eyes.

© Rachana Sood

Rachana Sood (Delhi, India)

rachanasekhri77@gmail.com

She is a bilingual poet who writes in English and Hindi languages. She writes under the name of 'Meethinimboli'. She is a member of various poetry groups on social media. She has contributed her poems to several anthologies, magazines, newspapers, and online-live poetry recitation events. Her writings are mainly concerned with diverse facets of human emotions and vibrant natural phenomena. She is B. A (Honours) in Tourism Studies. Currently, she is working as a Yoga owner and assisting her father in his construction company.

32. Exquisite Rose

Exquisite rose in the morning in color of memory,
Bright like sun in red face blushing over unplumbed sea,
Silently curls the petals in symmetry in the breeze,
The perfume in silence touching the breath anew,
I grow young as if I am changing the past into present.

She holds my eyes waiting to caress me as a bee,
I wait like a crane in the weedy pond looking for fish,
In the golden depth of morn till she comes to my hand,
Half-awakened in vision of love at first sight,
Enters into my shallow stream of blood for a storm.

How a rose blooms in hearts in tenderest care,
Though it may fade in the evening in time's fare,
A rose so lovely raptures my soul's delight,
Though its thorns and briers barred from its prize,
Love is always born in sweetest innocence of eyes.

© Rajendra K. Padhi

Rajendra K Padhi (Bhubaneswar, Odisha, India)

rajendrapadhi62@gmail.com

He is a poet, novelist, editor and translator. He has translated many stories, biographies and poems from Odia into English. He has written 5 books including poetry and novels. His articles, poems and interviews are published in more than 80 books, and journals from different countries of the world. He has been a keynote speaker address in both National and International conferences. He is retired as a Professor in English.

33. To My Valentine

It's the day meant to be for us my valentine,
It's only You who left me all alone again,
You and I are supposed to be together,
But fate never wanted us to be forever.

The entire world is feeling the fragrance of love,
From you my dear I never found any love,
If ever again I get a chance to feel the love,
It must not be you it had to be my first love.

I am having a relationship with loneliness,
It didn't leave me like you I must confess,
Poured all feelings of true love only on you,
You have left me void in this winter's dew.

I don't think you find a better one than me,
If at all you find me richer and more handsome than me,
If you have a chance of remembering me,
Follow your shadow you definitely find me.

© Rajesh Sharma Brahmabhatla

Rajesh Sharma Brahmabhatla

(Khammam, Telangana, India)

rajeshpa09@gmail.com

He is a bilingual poet. He writes in English and Telugu languages. He is an Admin of various poetry groups on Facebook. He has authored one English poetry book entitled 'Hey Honey'. His writings are part of several anthologies, newspapers and magazines. He has received many awards for his poetry. He is BSc in Computer Science and presently works for the Government of his state in the Panchaytraj Dept.

34. You Are My Life

I won't let you become someone else's
I've trusted your words
I've lost from your stubbornness
My soulmate I know
I'm the reason for your restlessness.

Don't hide your love
If you're in love then confess your love
I can't wait any longer
You're the craziest lover.

You can't be someone else's
We belong to each other
I am your life! You are my life.

© Ranjana Kashyap

Ranjana Kashyap (Jhakri, Himachal Pradesh, India)

ranj77in23@gmail.com

She is a poet, writer and artist. She is a member of various poetry groups on social media. She has contributed her poems to several anthologies, magazines, newspapers and blogs. Her paintings have been placed on various literary platforms. She is a passionate lover of nature. She holds the degree of M.A., B. Ed, ADCA and Art History. Presently, she is working as a professional painter.

35. Why Would Anyone Love Me?

I am neither an Actor nor a Doctor,
I am neither a billionaire nor an Engineer,
I was always amongst the children and young people,
I was always in the company of teachers.

With chalk and duster or cane in the hand,
I have no antics no charms, and no Charisma,
What is Unique and attractive in me?
Why would any woman fall for me?
Why would anyone Love me?

Some call me a tyrant and some a Dictator,
Some call me a scholar but some a Maverick,
Yet, many call me their mentor and their well-wisher.

Thousands of students and hundreds of Teachers,
Address me as 'Sir', respectfully and revere me,
They adore me as a role model and call me 'Teacher'.

© Ravi Thakur

Ravi Thakur (Hyderabad Telangana, India)

thakur.ravims@gmail.com

He is a a multi-lingual Poet who writes in languages--English, Hindi and Telugu languages. He has published an English Poetry Anthology titled 'Angel and Phoenix '. His poems are published in various National and International anthologies, newspapers and magazines. He is an active member of several poetry groups on Facebook. His major theme of poetry is contemporary Social issues. He is a post -graduate in Hindi Literature and Psychology. He is retired as Dist. Vocational Education Officer.

36. Because I Love You

I have placed a photo of us,
Not only on the study table,
Where I sit and write,
I have imprinted it in my heart.

The ditties we sang together,
Are not only recorded in gramophone,
They are my lifelines,
I hum them all the times.

Constant gazing into your irises,
Never tires me,
It rather infuses life in me,
As I read your unpronounced love for me.

Your embraces aren't enough,
To be entwined in you,
My soul and spirit,
Yearns for communion beyond this earthly love.
Not because I love doing it
Because…I love you, my dear, I love you.

© Ritu Kamra Kumar

Dr. Ritu Kamra Kumar (Yamunanagar, Haryana, India)

ritukumargmn@gmail.com

She is an avid writer, poet and academic. She has contributed more than 350 write-ups, articles and poems in several National newspapers and magazines and many research papers in National and International research journals and anthologies. She is the Editor in Chief of her College magazine. She has authored three books. She is M.A, M. Phil, and Ph.D. in English literature, and working as a HOD and Associate Professor in the Post graduate Department of English.

37. My Love

Hey dear!
Can't you hear ?
Your love could make me
Nothing except a teddy bear.

For you to play
In your sweet will and way
Not me
It is what they say.

Still I cheer
Dancing to your tune
Clapping with both hands
Like a teddy bear
Without shyness
Shame and fear
Can't you hear?

© Rohit Dash

Rohit Dash (Bargarah, Odisha, India)

rohitdash28@gmail.com

He is a multilingual poet and writer. He writes in Odia, English, Hindi and Sambalpuri languages. So far 24 of his books has been published. He is a member of various poetry groups on Facebook. His works are also published in many Jnternational anthologies and E-zines. He has received many awards and recognition for his poetry. He is M.A. in English and is retired as a Bank Manager.

38. Love What Thou Be So

Love, what thou be so?
An angel or a Jove or an Apollo that roams on,
On the Mountains, and on the Hills and on Cricks,
On the Plains and on the Plateaus'.

And in the Valley and in the Dyke thou be seen abode with
As a plant and as a Tree,
As a Herb and as a Shrub,
As a Bud, as an offshoot and as a Leaf.

All and all these forms,
Thy thyself weave them into a web called Nature,
Isn't it the very hue —Green be the sign of thou,
Flowers , Blossoms, Fragrance that bloom and blush upon be thy odour.

Admist , Bird, Beast, and Man,
Thou throb in the form of palpation,
But between the Lovers, who would cherish to be ideal
Thy be the union of the both Body and Soul

© Sane Shiva Shanker

Sane Shiva Shanker (Mahabubnagar, Telangana, India)

saneshivashankar@gmail.com

He is a poet and writer. He is a member of various poetry groups on social media. He has contributed many poems to several anthologies, magazines, newspapers, and blogs. He is M.A (Eng.), M Phill and B.Ed. By profession, he is a senior teacher in English.

39. Four Lettered Word

Love, a four-lettered word encapsulates the whole world,
Love, a fragrance that embalms the lover's heart,
Love, a feeling that enamors the lover's soul,
Love, like blossoms, keeps the soul in redolence.

Like ambrosia, love is food for the soul,
Love is kind, love is patient,
Love knows no foundation,
Love is pure joy, abounds.

Love binds in an unbreakable bond,
Love gives more than it takes,
Like the fragrance of the rose,
Love is a boon as beautiful as a moon.

Love may be from far,
But doesn't keep lovers apart,
Love is paradisiacal, love is an elysian,
It keeps our life alive.

© Seema Sharma

Seema Sharma (Delhi, India)

seemashar0807@gmail.com

She is a poet, writer and author. She is passionate about nature and reading books. She is a peace lover and believes in providing new horizons to her life. She is an active member of several literary platforms and participates in various literary activities. Her poems are part of several magazines, anthologies, and newspapers. She is a teacher by profession with MA in English.

40. Miracle of Love

Your lips wrote poetry of intimacy on my entire body,
Your eyes discovered secrets of my soul's rhapsody,
My heart melts with the enchantment of your voice,
The tenderness of your touch makes my pulse rise.

I seek your true love and care's amalgamation,
I crave more and more as much as I get your attention,
My dreams are always lit up with your bright presence,
Days seem to be dark in your unendurable absence.

I learned all the altered interpretations of fondness,
The warmth of emotions changes my anxiety to calmness,
A distinct pleasure to possess intense feelings,
Give new names to all dark desires and yearnings.

My shady world is astonished to discern a transformed me,
I erased my footprints from the shore of forlornness with glee,
Love is a rare miracle that encompasses only a few,
Not all the blossoms are kissed by the morning dew.

© Shafia Afzal

Shafia Afzal (Islamabad, Punjab, Pakistan)

afzalshafia5@gmail.com

She is a bilingual writer and poet. She writes in English and Urdu. Reading and writing have been her passion since childhood. She's a member of several renowned literary forums on social media. Her articles have been published in various National newspapers. She holds a degree of B.SC, in Statistics, Mathematics, and Economics.

41. Eternal Truth

Yes, No, Yes, No,
We confront in everyday life and Just forgo.
Love is a bond, Love is umbilical,
Love develops, Love stays strong.

As one grows, and observes,
Gets attracted and feels awed,
Reads discover that,
It is called love with the beloved.

Hey, I have found my Valentine,
Has now struck my mind,
Could not find an answer so far,
Late understanding is Absolutely fine.

Valentine is eternal truth,
Felt, touched by Heart, could not be uttered,
No matter what, the feeling is profound,
The truth will prevail….

And so Valentine will always be sound.

© Shelleyandra Kapil

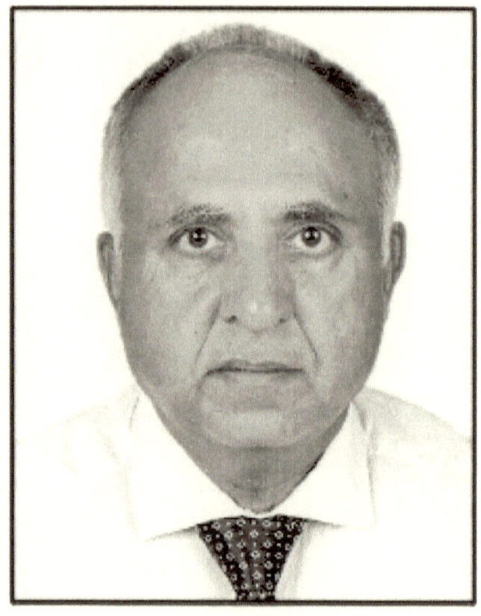

Shelleyandra Kapil (Chandigarh, India)

kapilirts@gmail.com

He is a poet, reviewer and writer, who writes in Hindi, Punjabi and English languages. He has published 6 books. His poems are published in various literary magazines, books, newspapers and anthologies. He has achieved several awards in his professional as well as literary fields. He is M.A in Public Administration. He has retired as Principal Chief Commercial Manager from North Central railways, Prayagraj.

42. The Unexpected Rain

The flow of water can't be stopped by a mere jerk.
What a lovely meadow of dream, created by the super hands,
She wondered, watching the sand bed under the moon.
And…I was also thinking of it, he added.

Lying on the smooth rock,
He had a futile attempt to…
count the stars above.

She also took part in it.
But, alas, an unexpected rain crept in to their calculations,
And gave wrong numbers,
Love story ended before it began.

© Sreedharan Parokode

Sreedharan Parokode (Kozhikode, Kerala, India)

sreeparokode@gmail.com

He is a bilingual poet and lyricist. He writes in English and Malayalam languages. He has thirty books of poems to his credit and has written songs for animation films also. His poems have been well received in different platforms and discussed. He presented his poems in various National and International platforms. He has received several awards and recognitions for his poetry. He beholds the degree of MA (Eco) M.A (Eng), M.A.(Popn Studies) M Phil and a Post Graduate Diploma in Parental Education. He is retired from Calicut University.

43. The Love Path

Is there a way that leads me away from thee?
If anyone finds one, do enlighten me.
I am so lost in the sweet intoxications of love,
That finding that way, no longer matters to me.

For you reside in every corner I frequent,
And in every unassailable task, I attempt.
Leading me to unimaginable destinations,
Am wonderstruck by the goodness, God has sent.

Be it angry waves crashing against the shore,
Or the lyrical ballads of ancient lore,
All seem to sing similar songs of love,
I mix it with my breath and into you, I pour.

If by fate, you are the chosen one for me
How do I deny God's honoured decree?
If way upon the way in life leads to you, my angel,
Maybe Death has a path, that leads me away from thee.

© Srividya Subramanian

Srividya Subramanian (Chennai, Tamil Nadu, India)

srivi1971@gmail.com

She is a poet, writer, and author. She writes poetry, stories, articles and essays. She is an active member of several literary platforms on social media. Her poems are part of several magazines, anthologies, and newspapers. Her other hobbies include cooking and listening to music. She is M.A. B. Ed. She is a teacher by profession. She has won a lot of recognition for her work.

44. My Dear Niece

I always wanted to have a baby girl,
Around whom my life will swirl,
But God gifted me with a baby boy,
And later, you came in my life as a bundle of joy.

My dear niece, you are so close to my heart,
That nothing can break us apart,
When your little fingers wrap around mine,
It plays my heart's strings and I feel divine.

When you are eager to come in my lap,
When we pose together for a snap,
When you don't want to be away from me,
Then I feel like on cloud nine, just like a honey bee.

You are an angel sent from heaven on earth,
Wrapped with joy and happiness, like a diamond placed in a casket,
You are like a sun, that is beaming and gleaming with joy,
You are my love, my valentine, with you every moment I enjoy.

© Dr. Suboohi Jafar

Dr. Suboohi Jafar (Varanasi, Uttar Pradesh, India)

suboohijafar@gmail.com

She is a young and dynamic poet, artist and singer by heart, an oncologist by profession. A Soldier in Fight against CANCER. She has won many awards and medals in her academic career. She has received several awards in poetry contests conducted by various poetic groups on Facebook.

45. A Lonely Bird

So lonely, I dwell on the verge of my life,
It's so unbearable, you see,
"Inside my confinement in the world of solitude,
Nobody misses me"
I wait for you in the deserted harbour of the endless sea.

Nobody appears at the dead-end of this situation,
Gone are the days of celebration,
Now, like a corpse of an unknown bird,
I hang on and wait for my end.

In my solitude, I crave affection
But everyone is here without any gratitude
In this toxic world, I need renunciation

So helpless I am!
Without any affinity, I survive like a barren land sans fertility
I wait, I long, I and realize:
In the solitary cage of my soul,
I am alone to resist the tormenting suffocation.

© Sudipta Mishra

Sudipta Mishra (Bhubaneshwar, Odisha, India)

sudiptamishra71@gmail.com

She is a multi-faceted artist and dancer excelling in various fields of art and culture. She has weaved more than a hundred books. Her book, 'The Essence of Life', is credited with Amazon bestseller, and 'The Songs of My Heart' is scaling newer heights of glory. She has garnered numerous accolades in literature, including the famous Rabindranath Tagore Memorial. She regularly pens articles in newspapers as a strong female voice. She is a research scholar, perusing a Ph.D. in English.

46. To the Wander-Lust Lover

The aroma of Spring is wafting in the air
and deadly chilly Winter days are gone;
The meadows are aflame with iridescent flowers
birds are singing on trees with sweet tones.

The fragrance of love is spreading like fire
men and women are frolicking recklessly on shore;
Preys of passion, they must be planning
a grand Valentine's celebration with fun galore.

Where are you darling, my long lost lover
in which country are you staying now?
My heart pines for your presence by my side
but you seem to have forgotten the sacred vow.

Come back home flying like migratory birds,
test not my patience like a hard taskmaster;
A few months of your company can rejuvenate me,
to distant lands then you are free to wander.

© Sulekha Samantaray

Sulekha Samantaray (Bhubaneshwar, Odisha, India)

sulekhasamantaray54@gmail.com

She is a bilingual writer with twelve published books and hundreds of articles including stories, poems, essays and translations both in English and Odia languages. She has also received many literary awards for her contribution to literature. She is M.A and M. Phil in English and retired as an Associate Professor in English.

47. Magical Gift

A treasure in the little heart,
Spreading a smile is an art,
Omnipresent like fragrance,
A friend during endurance.

Measureless in-depth of a sea,
Like a flower and bee,
A wick that spreads light and joy,
A feeling that makes you enjoy.

My absence makes one a monster,
My hug will foster,
Togetherness and close,
For I am a powerful force.

I am a fire,
Burning to fulfill the desire,
It's one thing in life we must pursue,
For its love that makes our life anew.

© Sulochana Narayanan

Sulochana Narayanan (Palakkad, Kerala, India)

sulsubra@gmail.com

She is a lover of arts like paintings, music and poetry. She has recently published her first book "Imprints: An Anthology of Poems". She is a member of various poetry groups on Facebook and has won several awards. She is M.A English and has done B.Ed. She is an academician by profession for the past 11 years.

48. O' My Beloved

In the core of my heart
You are a drop of
Heaven's dew.

A smile of moonlight.
A crystal wave of
Emerald sea.

And a gracious prayer
Of the universe
Embracing my soul
For years and years.

You, a divine dove.
On your wings of love
I fly in the mystical magical world.

An infinite joy I capture,
That divinity pervades
In our amorous desires
O' my beloved.

© Sumi Kapahera

Sumi Kapahera (Morigaon, Assam, India)

debend557@gmail.com

She is a poet by passion. At present, she is involved with many wonderful poetry platforms and literary organizations. She has achieved many awards including Gujarat Sahitya Academy certificates. She is an M.A. in English and BED, a teacher by profession.

49. The architecture in You

Show me the architecture in you and flowery terrace
For satisfaction of my thousand squirrelling eyes.
Your tempting finery is alluring me to be ravenous,
And it'll make me a dangerous rebel in disguise.

I wanted the fragrance of life from the jasmine
And enjoyed life's mellifluousness from each drop.
So I can't dishonour your shades and sheen
And your hidden staircases leading to the rooftop.

The grand opening in you will let me enter inside,
And the ruins will give me the company of your past.
I'll relearn the first experience without any guide—
By circumventing those ruins of your coloured dust.

But I'm not thriving to enter through your chaotic core
Or to recapture the screenshots of your bygone glory.
But I've noticed something precious or something more
Than the splendour in you; that has been preserved for me.

© Swapan Kumar Rakshit

Swapan Kumar Rakshit (Bankura, West Bengal, India)

rakshit.swapan2015@gmail.com

He is a poet and writer. His major genera of poetry is composing sonnets. He is a member of various literary groups on Facebook and actively participates in several contests. He has received many prizes for his poetry. His writings are the part of many newspapers, magazines and anthologies. He wants to be acquainted with the universal passionate minds of the poets. He is B. Sc. (Physics) B. Ed. M. A. and is working as a Physics teacher.

50. Forgotten Image

Blossoming pleasures pervade,
Salvo is her sincere presence.
Trumped up teeny bopper she is,
External love persists, nubile.

Throbbing heart, rhythmic drum,
Crimson faces stable shyness.
Jasmine-purity allures love,
Valentine's day is now recalled.

The invincible bond that ever exists,
Dreams stimulate in absence.
Silver electric rays in her eyes,
Damsel is incongruous in style.

Never present in the body, I dream,
A futile dream of unreal love.
Embezzled life, unreal image,
That image is ever fresh in me.

© **Unnikrishnan Atiyodi**

Unnikrishnan Atiyodi (Kannur, Kerala, India)

uatiyodi@gmail.com

He is a poet and writer with 3 collections of poems in English and also essays in English entitled 'Spectrum'. He has written three books in Malayalam and contributes regularly to e-journals. He is the winner of Sahithyamanjari Puraskaram. He is postgraduate in English and is retired as a principal of Higher Secondary school.

MELODIOUS MUSINGS OF LOVE

An Anthology of Poems
(Paperback, 1st Edition, February 2023)
Compiled & Edited BY
Dr. Sonia Gupta